Remember to live
each day "one at a time"...
to let go of things you cannot
change... and to keep in mind
that God is always with you
as He holds your heart
in His hands.

To my sister ♡

ISBN: 978-1-68088-411-1

Children of the Inner Light is a registered trademark. Used under license.

◰ and Blue Mountain Press are registered in U.S. Patent and Trademark Office. Certain trademarks are used under license.

Printed in China.
First Printing: 2022

⊕ This book is printed on recycled paper.

This book is printed on paper that has been specially produced to be acid free (neutral pH) and contains no groundwood or unbleached pulp. It conforms with the requirements of the American National Standards Institute, Inc., so as to ensure that this book will last and be enjoyed by future generations.

Blue Mountain Arts, Inc.

P.O. Box 4549, Boulder, Colorado 80306

Stay Strong

Every Challenge Has a Hidden Blessing

Marci

Blue Mountain Press™
Boulder, Colorado

Every
Challenge Has
a Hidden Blessing

When we are in the middle of a challenge, it can be hard to imagine that anything positive could come out of it. But in time, we come to realize that there is beauty in the strength we've seen in ourselves and that there are lessons we've learned, too — ones that can only be learned through experience.

Know that you will find the blessing in the challenges you face and look back at these times with a realization that now you have something wonderful to share with others — the beautiful gift of hope.

You Are Strong, You Are Brave

Even on the worst of days, everything you need to get through the day is right there for you.

You have a lot of wisdom inside, and if you don't know the answer, you have the skills to find it.

You are brave. You take a risk each time you put yourself out there to try something new or stand up for what you believe in. Courage is living with integrity.

You are strong. You've come through difficult times before and always emerged a better person. Be kind to yourself... be patient with yourself... and remember, strength is found in the words "I will."

When Your Journey Gets Difficult...

Remember to start each day with a prayer so your heart is open to the grace that comes your way.

See each struggle as an opportunity for enlightenment and growth.

Let go of things not meant for you, and focus on the choices in life that are yours.

Recognize the joy in the little things that are present to brighten every day.

Keep It Simple

God loves you♥ God loves
you♥ God loves you ♥
♥ God loves you ♥

Sometimes the challenges of life become more than we can take. These are times to remember that simple concepts help us keep our balance. Do the best you can one day at a time. Do not ask more of yourself than you can handle. And never forget that you are a child of God and you will be cared for in a way that you may only understand tomorrow!

God Is Always
Listening

Faith is the way

Often we forget to ask for help when we need it most. We get caught up in whatever is happening and forget that help is always available for the asking. That help is called "grace." It is always abundant... always accessible... and always exactly what we need. Remember, grace is only a prayer away.

Life is difficult; this is a fact. Spend energy learning to solve problems instead of trying to make life what it is not.

Remember that small actions and change in thinking can make a BIG difference... not necessarily in our circumstance, but in the way we feel.

The thoughts that we give
attention to enlarge... the fears
we dismiss lessen.

The door that closes behind you is
the one that opens your thinking
to new possibilities.

Realize the power in your choices,
and experience change in your life.

Everything Happens
for a Reason

So often we wonder about the "whys" in life... "Why did this happen?" "Why me?" "Why now?" But there is a secret that wise people know... Bumps in the road are an inevitable part of life that soften us, make us grow, and bestow upon us the virtue of compassion. Often it is only with the passing of time that it becomes clear that the cloud really did have a silver lining, and now we have wisdom, strength, and hope to share. And at last we understand the true meaning of the phrase "Everything happens for a reason."

All Things Will Come at the Right Time

There is a right time for everything. The universe teaches us this important concept with its order. There is a sunrise and a sunset... Days turn into weeks and weeks into months... There are tides that ebb and flow with the rhythm and timing written long ago... And so it is with our lives. Have faith that a power greater than yourself knows what is best for you... and when.

This, Too, Shall Pass

HOPE

When life sends difficult times, along with them comes the feeling that no one could possibly understand what we are going through. We want to find a way to feel better, but we can't seem to find the path.

In these times, remember that you are never alone. God always hears our prayers, even when we can't hear the answers. There are others who have experienced similar things, so reach out and grab the gift of encouragement. Open your heart to the kindness of others, and always keep this truth in mind... This, too, shall pass.

As You Follow Life's Path, Remember...

No matter where life takes you or what path you choose, you will always meet challenges. That is the way life is. There are no guarantees, and no matter how many things you do right or how many rules you follow, there will always be that fork in the road that makes you choose between this way or that. Whenever you meet this place, remember these things: You are loved... love will sustain you. You are strong... prayer will get you through anything. You are wise... the greatest gift of all lies within you.

Some Simple Thoughts to Help You Get Through Anything

We all have those days when everything feels all wrong — and it's really hard to put our thoughts into words. On these days, remember to...

Take a deep breath. Breathe in positive energy; breathe out negative thoughts.

Just ride the wave. Often, these times of mental turmoil signify the process of acceptance taking place in our inner world. Trust the process.

Shift from thinking to action. Release energy through exercise, music, chores, or a walk.

Reach out and connect. Call a friend or family member just to say hello, or enjoy a connection with a stranger while shopping.

Take in all the encouragement you can, and remember... some days, all you need is a hug!

There Is So Much More to Life Than We Can See

In childhood we do not understand the gifts wrapped up in a Greater Plan... but time and the living of life carve into our souls an attitude of acceptance and understanding. Adulthood brings an appreciation of all the gifts we've been given and a realization that some of the most valuable gifts are the ones we labeled as losses.

The universe has chosen for us — or perhaps we have selected for ourselves — the path we needed to become whole. Sometimes we followed... sometimes we resisted, only to circle back around to the lessons left unlearned. One day... after a big storm... a rainbow appears... and we find the sky is bright with a beautiful realization that everything "is as it should be" in this wonderful miracle called life.

FAITH

HOPE

LOVE

You Already Have Everything You Need to Succeed

Love is the greatest gift of all.

Everything you need to succeed in this life is right inside you. It is the joy that comes with the discovery of your God-given talents, which will come forth at just the right time. It is the belief that you can overcome all the challenges that come with navigating this journey of life. It is the realization that through whatever life hands you, you will always know that love is what matters most of all.

Wisdom Is a Gift That Comes Through Experience

Often, it is through our struggles that we gain the most understanding. We learn about who we are, what we believe, and what is really important through everyday living. When we meet the challenge to change and grow spiritually, accepting our joys and sorrows with gratitude, we become wise and our days will be filled with experiences that enrich our lives!

Let Your Inner Compass Guide You

On the days when you wonder about decisions you need to make... when you ask yourself which path to take... remember, let your inner compass guide you.

There is a wisdom there that will help you find your North Star. There's a quiet voice that's leading the way and guiding you toward the light that shines with the insights you need to navigate that fork in the road. Ask for guidance, and trust the knowledge deep inside your heart. Listen for the truth when you are in quiet reflection. Keep your intentions aligned with what is good, and trust that you will find your way.

The Important Things in Life Aren't Things

We often look at successful people and expect them to be happy because they have "everything that money can buy." But if we speak to the wise or the elderly, they tell us that life has taught them an important truth: Real treasures are not found in a chest of gold... or even in a dream at the end of a rainbow... but are captured in those tiny moments that live in our memories.

These moments are created by the
simple things... a walk... a talk...
a laugh... and through our connection,
we experience the priceless things...
wisdom... hope... and love. Finally
we realize that these are the gems
that are ours to keep
forever, and we
acknowledge
our fortune and
say: "We have
everything that
money CAN'T buy!"

The Path to Happiness

* Pay attention to what you feed your mind. Make a decision to read some inspirational material every day.

* Say NO to negative thoughts. Time and a commitment to this practice will change the way you feel as you meet the challenges of life.

* Be a positive force in the lives of others. Share what is good and happy in your life. Remember, happiness is contagious. What you send out will come right back to you!

* Make time for people who love you.

* Put toxic people out of your life.

* When you need a pick-me-up, find
  someone who needs a little wisdom,
  hope, and strength — share...
  and listen.

* Watch for angels...
  They are everywhere.

* End the day with a
  prayer of thanksgiving.

Stay Strong, and the Gifts of Wisdom and Hope Will Be Yours

Sometimes we feel powerless as we struggle to make sense of the world and try to figure out what we can do to make life better — but real power is found in our choices and the decisions we make about how to cope.

Stay strong... keep positive — and one day you'll look back at all you've gone through and realize that you now have something powerful to share... the gifts of wisdom and hope.

About Marci

Marci began her career by hand painting floral designs on clothing. No one was more surprised than she was when one day, in a single burst of inspiration and a completely new and different art style, her delightful characters sprang from her pen! "Their wild and crazy hair is a sign of strength," she thought, "and their crooked little smiles are endearing." She quickly identified the charming characters as Mother, Daughter, Sister, Father, Son, Friend, and so on until all the people and places in life were filled. Then, with her own loved ones in mind, she wrote a true and special sentiment to each one. This would be the beginning of a wonderful success story, which today still finds Marci writing each and every one of her verses in this same personal way.

Marci is a self-taught artist who has always enjoyed writing and art. She is thrilled to see how her delightful characters and universal messages of love have touched the hearts and lives of people everywhere. Her distinctive designs can also be found on Blue Mountain Arts greeting cards, calendars, bookmarks, and other gift items.

To learn more about Marci, look for Children of the Inner Light on Facebook or visit her website: www.MARCIonline.com.